FINDING YOUR DHARMA IN PRODUCT MANAGEMENT

GUIDANCE FROM THE BHAGAVAD GITA

KUMAR VISHWESH

Made with ❤ on the Notion Press Platform
www.notionpress.com

Contents

Contents

Preface

The Bhagavad Gita is a revered Hindu scripture that has gained a following in the field of product management for its practical and holistic approach to decision-making and problem-solving. This book outlines how the principles of the Gita, such as the idea of selfless action, the concept of dharma, and the importance of surrendering the ego, can be applied to the challenges faced by product managers. It also discusses the relevance of the Gita's teachings in maintaining balance and clarity in the face of difficult situations. By incorporating the wisdom of the Gita into their work, product managers can approach their role with a greater sense of purpose and fulfillment. Whether you are new to product management or an experienced professional, this book will provide you with valuable insights and guidance that can help you to lead and create with purpose and integrity.

Preface

The Bhagavad Gita is a revered Hindu scripture that has gained a following in the field of product management for its practical and holistic approach to decision-making and problem-solving. This book outlines how the principles of the Gita, such as the idea of selfless action, the concept of dharma, and the importance of surrendering the ego, can be applied to the challenges faced by product managers. It also discusses the relevance [illegible] challenges in maintaining balance and [illegible] [illegible] their work, product managers [illegible] with a greater sense of [illegible] [illegible] product management [illegible] professional, this book will provide you with valuable insights and guidance that can help you to lead and create with purpose and integrity.

Introduction

CHAPTER ONE

The Bhagavad Gita as a spiritual text and its relevance in the field of product management

The Bhagavad Gita is a spiritual text that has gained widespread popularity around the world for its profound insights on the human condition and the path to enlightenment. It is a central text in Hinduism and is considered to be one of the greatest works of spiritual wisdom in the world. In this chapter, we will explore the Bhagavad Gita's relevance in the field of product management.

* * *

The Principle of Selfless Action

One of the key themes of the Bhagavad Gita is the importance of acting selflessly, without the desire for personal gain. This principle, known as "karma yoga," suggests that true happiness and fulfillment come from being detached from the outcomes of our actions and simply focusing on the act of doing. In product management, the principle of selfless action can help us to let go of our ego and focus on the needs of the customer and the team.

* * *

The Concept of Dharma

Another key concept in the Bhagavad Gita is the idea of dharma, which refers to one's moral and ethical duties in life. In product management, it is important to consider the impact of our products on society and to act in accordance with our values and principles.

* * *

Surrendering the Ego

The Bhagavad Gita teaches that true fulfillment comes from letting go of the ego and acting with humility and selflessness. In product management, this means letting go of the need for recognition or praise and instead focusing on the needs of the customer and the team.

* * *

Disciplining the mind and senses

Finally, the Bhagavad Gita emphasizes the importance of disciplining the mind and senses as a path to inner peace and fulfillment. In product management, disciplining the mind and senses can help us to stay focused and centered, and to make better decisions.

* * *

Conclusion

The teachings of the Bhagavad Gita have much to offer those working in the field of product management. By incorporating the principles of selfless action, dharma, surrendering the ego, and disciplining the mind and senses into our work, we can create more value for ourselves and others and find greater fulfillment in our work.

* * *

The Principle of Selfless Action

CHAPTER TWO

Acting without attachment to the fruits of one's actions can be applied to product management

The Bhagavad Gita is a spiritual text that has much to offer those working in the field of product management. One of its central teachings is the importance of acting without attachment to the fruits of one's actions, a principle known as "karma yoga."

* * *

The Gita's Teaching of Karma Yoga

According to the Gita, true happiness and fulfillment come from being detached from the outcomes of our actions and simply focusing on the act of doing. This principle has much to offer product managers in today's fast-paced, results-driven business world, where it can be easy to become overly attached to the outcomes of our work.

* * *

How to Apply Karma Yoga in Product Management

So, how can we apply the Gita's teaching of acting without attachment to the fruits of our actions in product management? Here are a few ways:

- **Focus on the process, not the outcome:** As product managers, it's easy to get caught up in the constant pursuit of success and to become overly focused on the end result. However, the Gita teaches us to let go of our attachment to specific outcomes and to focus on the process of creating value. This means being present in the moment and focusing on the task at hand, rather than constantly worrying about the end result.
- **Let go of the ego:** The Gita teaches that true fulfillment comes from letting go of the ego and acting with humility and selflessness. In product management, this means letting go of the need for recognition or praise and instead focusing on the needs of the customer and the team.
- **Practice gratitude:** The Gita teaches that true happiness comes from being grateful for what we have, rather than constantly striving for more. In product management, this means taking the time to appreciate the small wins and to be thankful for the opportunities we have been given.

* * *

Conclusion

By incorporating the principles of karma yoga into our work, we can become more focused, selfless, and grateful, and ultimately create more value for ourselves and others.

* * *

CHAPTER THREE

The importance of focusing on the needs of the user and the greater good in product management

As product managers, our ultimate goal is to create products that are valuable and useful to our customers. However, it is also important to consider the needs of the user and the greater good when making decisions about the direction of a product.

* * *

The Needs of the User

At the heart of every successful product is a deep understanding of the needs and wants of the user. As product managers, it is our responsibility to continually gather feedback and insights from customers and to use this information to inform our product roadmap and decisions. By putting the needs of the user at the center of our work, we can create products that truly meet the needs of our customers.

* * *

The Greater Good

In addition to considering the needs of the user, it is also important to consider the impact of our products on the greater good. This means considering the ethical and societal implications of our products and making sure that we are creating value for all stakeholders, not just shareholders.

* * *

How to Balance the Needs of the User and the Greater Good

So, how can we balance the needs of the user and the greater good in product management? Here are a few tips:

- **Gather feedback from a diverse group of users:** It is important to gather feedback from a diverse group of users to ensure that our products are meeting the needs of a wide range of people.
- **Consider the broader impact of our products:** As we make decisions about the direction of our products, it is important to consider the potential impact on the greater good.

- **Communicate transparently:** It is important to be transparent about the decisions we are making and the reasons behind them. This helps to build trust with our customers and stakeholders.

* * *

Conclusion

By focusing on the needs of the user and the greater good, we can create products that are truly valuable and impactful.

* * *

The Concept of Dharma

CHAPTER FOUR

How the Gita's concept of one's moral and ethical duties can be applied to product management

The Bhagavad Gita is a spiritual text that has much to offer those working in the field of product management. One of its central concepts is the idea of dharma, which refers to one's moral and ethical duties in life. In this chapter, we will explore how the Gita's concept of dharma can be applied to product management.

* * *

What is Dharma?

According to the Bhagavad Gita, dharma refers to the inherent nature of something and the role it plays in the natural order of the universe. In the context of product management, dharma can be thought of as the moral and ethical duties that we have in relation to the products we create.

* * *

How to Apply the Concept of Dharma in Product Management

So, how can we apply the concept of dharma in product management? Here are a few ways:

- **Consider the impact of our products on society:** As product managers, it is our responsibility to consider the potential impact of our products on society and to act in accordance with our values and principles.
- **Foster transparency:** By being transparent about the decisions we are making and the reasons behind them, we can build trust with our customers and stakeholders and demonstrate our commitment to ethical practices.
- **Prioritize sustainability:** The concept of dharma reminds us to consider the long-term impact of our products on the environment and to prioritize sustainability in our decision-making.

* * *

Conclusion

The concept of dharma as outlined in the Bhagavad Gita can be a powerful guiding principle for product managers. By considering the impact of our products on society, fostering transparency, and prioritizing sustainability, we can create products that are not only valuable and useful to our customers, but also aligned with our values and ethical responsibilities.

* * *

CHAPTER FIVE

Creating products that align with company values and have a positive impact on society

As product managers, our ultimate goal is to create products that are valuable and useful to our customers. However, it is also important to consider how our products align with our company's values and how they impact society. In this chapter, we will explore the importance of creating products that align with company values and have a positive impact on society in product management.

* * *

Why Align Products with Company Values?

Aligning our products with our company's values is important for a number of reasons. First, it helps to build trust with our customers and stakeholders. By demonstrating that our products are aligned with our values and mission, we can show that we are committed to creating value for all stakeholders, not just shareholders. Additionally, aligning our products with our values helps to create a sense of purpose and meaning in our work, which can be motivating and fulfilling.

* * *

The Importance of Creating Products with a Positive Impact on Society

In addition to aligning our products with our company's values, it is also important to consider the impact of our products on society. This means considering the ethical and societal implications of our products and making sure that we are creating value for all stakeholders, not just shareholders. By creating products that have a positive impact on society, we can not only create value for our customers, but also contribute to the greater good.

* * *

How to Create Products that Align with Company Values and Have a Positive Impact on Society

So, how can we create products that align with our company's values and have a positive impact on society? Here are a few tips:

- **Clearly define your company's values:** It is important to clearly define your company's values so that you can use them as a guide in your product development decisions.
- **Gather feedback from a diverse group of stakeholders:** It is important to gather feedback from a diverse group of stakeholders, including customers, employees, and community members, to ensure that your products are aligned with your values and are having a positive impact on society.
- **Communicate transparently:** By being transparent about the decisions you are making and the reasons behind them, you can build trust with your customers and stakeholders and demonstrate your commitment to ethical practices.

* * *

Conclusion

Creating products that align with company values and have a positive impact on society is important for building trust, creating meaning in our work, and contributing to the greater good. By following these tips, product managers can create products that are not only valuable and useful to customers, but also aligned with our values and ethical responsibilities.

* * *

Surrendering the Ego

CHAPTER SIX

The Gita's emphasis on letting go of the ego and focusing on a higher purpose

The Bhagavad Gita is a spiritual text that teaches the importance of letting go of the ego and focusing on a higher purpose. In this chapter, we will explore the Gita's emphasis on letting go of the ego and how it can be applied in our daily lives.

* * *

What is the Ego?

According to the Gita, the ego is the part of our consciousness that is focused on our own personal desires and needs. It is the source of our feelings of separation and individuality, and can lead us to act out of selfish motives.

* * *

The Importance of Letting Go of the Ego

The Gita teaches that true fulfillment and inner peace come from letting go of the ego and focusing on a higher purpose. By letting go of our ego, we can become more selfless and focused on serving others, rather than constantly seeking personal gain.

* * *

How to Let Go of the Ego

So, how can we let go of the ego and focus on a higher purpose? Here are a few tips:

- **Practice self-reflection:** By taking the time to reflect on our motivations and actions, we can become more aware of when the ego is driving our behavior.
- **Practice gratitude:** Focusing on the things we are grateful for can help us to let go of our ego and focus on the present moment.
- **Serve others:** By serving others, we can let go of our ego and focus on the needs of others rather than our own desires.
- **Practice mindfulness:** By practicing mindfulness, we can become more present in the moment and let go of our ego's constant need for recognition and validation.

* * *

Conclusion

The Gita's emphasis on letting go of the ego and focusing on a higher purpose is a powerful reminder that true fulfillment and inner peace come from letting go of our ego and focusing on serving others. By incorporating these practices into our daily lives, we can let go of our ego and find greater meaning and purpose in our lives.

* * *

CHAPTER SEVEN

The benefits of working towards the success of the product and the company as a whole

As product managers, our ultimate goal is to create successful products that meet the needs of our customers and drive business results. However, it is also important to consider the success of the company as a whole. In this chapter, we will explore the benefits of working towards the success of the product and the company as a whole in product management.

* * *

Why Focus on the Success of the Product and the Company?

There are many benefits to focusing on the success of both the product and the company as a whole. First, it helps to create a sense of purpose and meaning in our work. By working towards the success of the product and the company, we can feel like we are contributing to something larger than ourselves and making a positive impact. Additionally, focusing on the success of the product and the company can lead to greater job satisfaction and career

* * *

How to Focus on the Success of the Product and the Company

So, how can we focus on the success of the product and the company in product management? Here are a few tips:

- **Stay aligned with business goals:** It is important to stay aligned with the business goals of the company and to understand how your product fits into the overall strategy.
- **Communicate effectively:** By communicating effectively with all stakeholders, you can ensure that everyone is working towards the same goals and that the product is meeting the needs of the customer and driving business results.
- **Foster teamwork and collaboration:** By fostering teamwork and collaboration, you can create a positive and supportive work environment that is focused on the success of the product and the company as a whole.
- **Continuously gather feedback and insights:** By continuously gathering feedback and insights from customers and other stakeholders, you can ensure that

your product is meeting the needs of the market and driving business results.

* * *

Conclusion

Focusing on the success of the product and the company as a whole has many benefits for product managers. By staying aligned with business goals, communicating effectively, fostering teamwork and collaboration, and continuously gathering feedback and insights, we can create successful products that drive business results and contribute to the overall success of the company.

* * *

Disciplining the mind and senses

CHAPTER EIGHT

The Gita's teachings on disciplining the mind and senses

The Bhagavad Gita is an ancient Sanskrit text that is considered to be one of the most important works of Hindu philosophy. Within its pages, the Gita offers a wide range of teachings on how to live a fulfilling and meaningful life. One key theme of the Gita is the importance of disciplining the mind and senses in order to attain self-control and inner peace. In this chapter, we will explore the Gita's teachings on this topic and how they can be applied in modern life.

* * *

The Importance of Disciplining the Mind and Senses

According to the Gita, the mind and senses are like wild horses that need to be tamed and controlled in order to reach our full potential. When our mind and senses are undisciplined, they can lead us astray and cause us to make poor decisions that harm ourselves and others. By disciplining the mind and senses, we can gain greater control over our thoughts and actions, leading to a more peaceful and harmonious life.

* * *

The Role of Meditation in Disciplining the Mind and Senses

One of the key tools for disciplining the mind and senses, according to the Gita, is meditation. Through the practice of meditation, we can learn to quiet the noise of the mind and focus our attention on a single point, such as the breath or a mantra. This helps us to develop greater awareness of our thoughts and emotions, and to see them for what they are rather than getting caught up in them. Over time, regular meditation can help us to gain greater control over our mind and senses, leading to a calmer and more centered state of being.

* * *

The Connection Between Disciplining the Mind and Senses and Attaining Enlightenment

The Gita teaches that the ultimate goal of life is to attain enlightenment, or union with the divine. According to the Gita, this state of enlightenment can only be reached by disciplining the mind and senses and freeing ourselves from attachments and desires. By taming the mind and senses and focusing our attention inward, we can gain greater insight into the true nature of reality and our place within it. This understanding can lead to a state of inner peace and harmony, and the realization of our full potential as human beings.

* * *

Conclusion

In conclusion, the Gita's teachings on disciplining the mind and senses offer a powerful and practical guide for living a more fulfilling and meaningful life. Whether through the practice of meditation or other means, disciplining the mind and senses can help us to gain greater control over our thoughts and actions, leading to a more peaceful and harmonious state of being.

* * *

CHAPTER NINE

Disciplining the mind and senses can be useful in maintaining clarity and balance

In this chapter, we will explore how the Gita's teachings on disciplining the mind and senses can be useful for product managers in maintaining clarity and balance in difficult situations.

* * *

The Challenges of Being a Product Manager

Product management is a demanding and often stressful role that requires a high level of focus, decision-making skills, and the ability to manage competing priorities. Product managers are faced with a constant stream of challenges, including tight deadlines, changing market conditions, and the need to balance the needs of different stakeholders. In this fast-paced and high-pressure environment, it is easy for product managers to lose sight of their goals and become overwhelmed by their responsibilities.

* * *

The Role of Disciplining the Mind and Senses in Maintaining Clarity and Balance

According to the Gita, disciplining the mind and senses is essential for attaining self-control and inner peace. This is particularly relevant for product managers, who must maintain a clear and focused mind in order to make sound decisions and stay on track. By disciplining the mind and senses, product managers can gain greater control over their thoughts and emotions, allowing them to stay calm and centered even in the face of difficult situations. This can help them to maintain clarity and balance in their work, leading to better outcomes for their products and their teams.

* * *

Practical Strategies for Disciplining the Mind and Senses

So how can product managers put the Gita's teachings on disciplining the mind and senses into practice in their work? Here are a few strategies that may be helpful:

- **Practice meditation or other mindfulness techniques:** These practices can help product managers to quiet the noise of the mind and focus their attention on the present moment. This can help them to gain greater clarity and perspective on their work, and to make better decisions.

- **Set clear goals and priorities:** By establishing clear goals and priorities, product managers can stay focused on what is most important and avoid becoming overwhelmed by distractions.
- **Take breaks and practice self-care:** It is important for product managers to take breaks and practice self-care in order to maintain their physical and mental health. This can help them to stay energized and focused, and to better handle the challenges of their work.
- **Foster a culture of selflessness and compassion:** Product managers can encourage their teams to embrace the Gita's teachings on selflessness and compassion, leading to a more positive and collaborative work environment.
- **Seek out opportunities for personal growth and self-reflection:** Product managers can use the Gita's teachings as a guide for personal growth and self-reflection, leading to greater fulfillment and meaning in their work and their lives.

* * *

Conclusion

In conclusion, the Gita's teachings on disciplining the mind and senses can be highly useful for product managers in maintaining clarity and balance in difficult situations. By putting these teachings into practice, product managers can gain greater control over their thoughts and emotions, leading to better outcomes for their products and their teams.

* * *

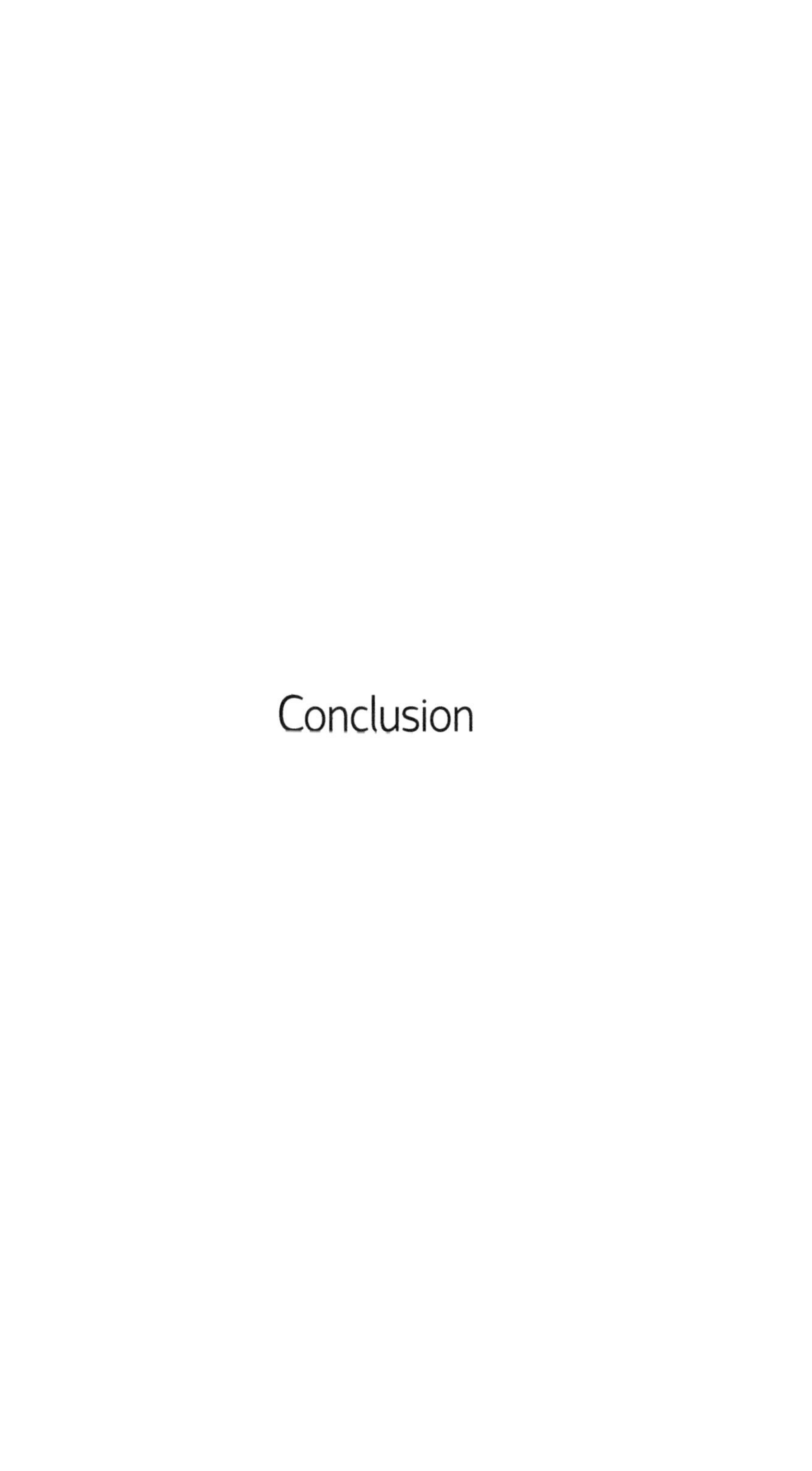

Conclusion

CHAPTER TEN

The benefits of incorporating the principles of the Bhagavad Gita into product management

The Bhagavad Gita is an ancient Sanskrit text that is considered to be one of the most important works of Hindu philosophy. Within its pages, the Gita offers a wide range of teachings on how to live a fulfilling and meaningful life, including the importance of self-control, discipline, and inner peace. In this chapter, we will explore the benefits of incorporating the principles of the Gita into product management.

* * *

The Principles of the Gita and Their Relevance to Product Management

The Gita teaches that the ultimate goal of life is to attain enlightenment, or union with the divine. According to the Gita, this state of enlightenment can only be reached by disciplining the mind and senses, freeing ourselves from attachments and desires, and living in accordance with our highest values. These principles are highly relevant to product management, where discipline, focus, and the ability to let go of attachments are key to success.

* * *

The Benefits of Incorporating the Gita's Teachings into Product Management

So what are the benefits of incorporating the Gita's teachings into product management? Here are a few examples:

- **Greater clarity and focus:** By disciplining the mind and senses and living in accordance with our highest values, product managers can gain greater clarity and focus on their work, leading to better decision-making and improved outcomes.
- **Increased creativity and innovation:** The Gita teaches that true creativity and innovation come from a state of inner peace and stillness. By incorporating the Gita's teachings into their work, product managers can tap into this inner wellspring of creativity and bring new and innovative ideas to their products.

- **Improved team morale and collaboration:** The Gita's teachings on selflessness and compassion can help product managers to create a more positive and collaborative work environment, leading to increased morale and improved teamwork.
- **Personal growth and fulfillment:** By living in accordance with the Gita's teachings, product managers can gain greater personal growth and fulfillment in their work and their lives.

* * *

Conclusion

In conclusion, the principles of the Gita can be highly beneficial for product managers looking to improve their work and their lives. By incorporating these teachings into their work, product managers can gain greater clarity, focus, and creativity, and create a more positive and collaborative work environment.

* * *

CHAPTER ELEVEN

The potential for a more holistic and purpose-driven approach & personal fulfillment

Product management is an integral part of any successful business, but it can often be a challenging and stressful role. Many product managers are focused on meeting deadlines, hitting targets, and driving revenue, which can lead to a narrow and purely profit-driven approach to product development. However, there is a growing recognition of the potential for a more holistic and purpose-driven approach to creating and managing products, which not only delivers financial success but also has a positive impact on society and the environment. This shift in focus is driven by a number of factors, including the increasing importance of sustainability and social responsibility, the rise of the purpose-driven consumer, and the recognition that a more meaningful and fulfilling work experience can lead to better outcomes for both the business and its employees.

* * *

Personal Fulfillment in the Product Manager Role

In addition to the potential for a more purpose-driven approach to product management, there is also the opportunity for personal fulfillment in the role. Product management can be a rewarding career for those who are passionate about creating and bringing new products to market, and who enjoy the challenges and problem-solving that come with it. However, it is important for product managers to find a sense of meaning and purpose in their work, and to feel that they are making a positive contribution to the world. This can be achieved through aligning their personal values and goals with those of the company, and by actively seeking out opportunities to make a positive impact through their work. For example, product managers can look for ways to incorporate sustainability and social responsibility into their product development processes, or to create products that address pressing societal challenges such as climate change or inequality. By doing so, they can find a greater sense of fulfillment and satisfaction in their work, while also contributing to the greater good.

* * *

Conclusion

The product management role is an essential and influential one within any business, and there is a growing recognition of the potential for a more holistic and purpose-driven approach to creating and managing products. This shift not only has the potential to drive financial success, but also to create a more meaningful and fulfilling work experience for product managers, and to make a positive impact on society and the environment. By aligning their personal values and goals with those of the company, and actively seeking out opportunities to make a positive impact, product managers can find a greater sense of fulfillment and satisfaction in their work.

9 798890 021168

Printed by Libri Plureos GmbH in Hamburg,
Germany